Investigating Child Fatalities

Portable Guides to Investigating Child Abuse

Office of Justice Programs
Partnerships for Safer Communities
www.ojp.usdoj.gov

Office of Juvenile Justice and Delinquency Prevention
www.ojp.usdoj.gov/ojjdp

August 2005

Contents

Every year in the United States, tens of thousands of children die from a variety of causes, including illnesses, diseases, accidents, suicides, and homicides. Each death is a heartbreaking event for the child's family and a tragic loss for society. When a child's death is sudden and unexpected, the tragedy is compounded if law enforcement fails to conduct a proper investigation. If the investigation is flawed, two outcomes—neither acceptable—are very real possibilities. The first is that an innocent person will be suspected or accused of either a crime that did not occur or a crime for which the person bears no responsibility. The other possibility is that a real crime will remain undetected or unsolved, and the person responsible for the fatal maltreatment of the child will never be identified or prosecuted.

Overview

Although the vast majority of child deaths are related to natural causes or accidents, all sudden and unexpected child deaths must be properly investigated. This guide defines a sudden and unexpected death as any death that was not caused by a known disease or illness for which the child was under a physician's care at the time of death. Included in this category are deaths believed to be the result of Sudden Infant Death Syndrome (SIDS), accidents, suicides, homicides, and undetermined circumstances. The guide uses the term **"child fatality investigation"** for the law enforcement inquiry into the death of a child in which investigators believe abuse or neglect caused or contributed to the fatal injury. This convention is consistent with the definition that the National Child Abuse and Neglect Data System uses. The guide uses the term **"maltreatment"** to indicate child abuse or neglect.

The main purpose of this portable guide is to provide practical information for law enforcement officers investigating child fatality cases. The guide will also be useful for child protective service investigators, prosecutors, child fatality review team members, and other professionals involved in these cases. Although the guide presents information relevant to investigating all types of cases involving the sudden and unexpected death of a child, the focus is on child fatalities as defined above, in the term "child fatality investigations."

Today, while you are reading this guide, at least four children in the United States will die from maltreatment. Experience has shown that only by thoroughly investigating all sudden and unexpected child deaths can we be certain that maltreatment is not involved. Professionally conducted investigations of child fatalities ensure that innocent people are not falsely accused of wrongdoing and guilty people are not allowed to escape justice and possibly harm another child. In these cases, your responsibility as the principal law enforcement investigator is to determine what happened to the child and who, if anyone, is responsible. This guide provides practical information needed to perform these important tasks.

The Nature of Child Fatality Cases

Awareness of some basic dynamics and issues is critical to effective investigations of child fatalities. Research and experience have shown that children are most at risk of dying of maltreatment during the first 4 years of life. In fact, 40 percent of children who are victims of fatal maltreatment are infants (younger than 1 year old) and 75 percent are younger than 5 years old. The Centers for Disease Control and Prevention have reported that the chances of being murdered are greater on the day of birth than at any other point in a person's life. Caring for children during their preschool years can be very stressful for parents and other caretakers. Faced with a young child's persistent problems with sleeping, feeding, and toilet-training, a caretaker may lose control and assault the child in anger or may cause injury while punishing the child. Some inexperienced caretakers have unrealistic expectations about what is appropriate child behavior and what children are even capable of doing in the early stages of their development. Some caretakers become angry because they view a child's crying or bedwetting as an act of defiance rather than as normal behavior for a young child. The deadly combination of an angry adult and a physically vulnerable child can result in fatal or life-threatening injuries to the child.

The majority of child fatalities can be categorized as a variation of either acute or chronic maltreatment. The next sections discuss the characteristics of these categories.

Acute Maltreatment

Acute maltreatment means that the child's death is directly related to injuries suffered as a result of a specific incident of abuse or act of negligence. Often in such cases, the child has not been previously abused or neglected.

In cases involving acute physical abuse, the caretaker may have fatally assaulted the child in either an inappropriate response to the child's behavior or a conscious act to hurt the child. Offenders in cases of Shaken Baby Syndrome (SBS), in which a child's brain is injured from violent shaking, often cite the child's crying as the "triggering event."

In cases of acute neglect, a caretaker's one-time failure to properly supervise the child may result in a fatal injury. A common example is a fatal drowning that occurs when a parent leaves an infant briefly unsupervised in a bathtub. Far too often, children sustain fatal gunshot wounds when caretakers fail to properly secure loaded firearms. Some states have statutes that specifically assign criminal responsibility to an individual who makes a firearm accessible to a child, either intentionally or through failure to properly secure the weapon. The penalty for this crime may be increased if the child's possession of the firearm results in either injury or death to the child or another.

Chronic Maltreatment

In chronic maltreatment cases, the child's death is directly related to injuries caused by abuse and/or neglect occurring over an extended period. Battered Child Syndrome is an example of chronic physical abuse. Although the direct cause of death in a battering case is usually a single specific injury (often brain trauma), numerous indications of previous maltreatment—old and new injuries and possible signs of neglect—are usually present. Depriving a child of food for a significant period of time is a common form of chronic physical neglect. In cases of chronic abuse or neglect, a history of the child's previous maltreatment often will appear in either Child Protective Services (CPS) or medical records. In fact, in 2000, 38 percent of all children who died of abuse or neglect had prior or current contact with a CPS agency.

How Child Fatalities Differ From Other Types of Homicide Cases

Everyone involved in the investigation of a child fatality must understand that these cases differ from typical homicides in many ways, including the causes of death, the offender's motivations and legal culpability for the crime, the methods used to inflict the fatal injuries, the types of injuries that the victim sustained, the forensic and physical evidence involved, and the investigative techniques used. The following sections discuss some of the unique issues you may encounter in child fatality cases.

Delayed Death

Many maltreatment deaths involve a delay between the time the child sustains the fatal injury and the subsequent death of the child. Although this may also be true with any serious injury, it commonly happens in cases of abusive head trauma (AHT) and in cases involving internal injuries to the chest and abdomen. (AHT, the most common type of fatal injury in maltreatment deaths, includes brain trauma resulting from SBS and other types of direct blunt trauma to the brain.) In fact, you often will be called to the hospital about a severely injured child being treated or surviving on a life support system and learn that the prognosis for survival is slim. Depending on the injuries sustained, that child may survive anywhere from hours to days.

This delayed death scenario can also occur when a child is severely scalded from an immersion burn, suffers an infection or other medical complications arising from the injuries, and then dies weeks or months after the incident occurred. Or a child may suffer severe brain trauma and lapse into a coma for months, only to die eventually from pneumonia or some other medical complication. Although the abuse was not the immediate cause of death in these situations, the manner of death would still most likely be ruled a homicide because the original abuse was the basis for the medical complication that resulted in death.

Witnesses and Accomplices

Another common factor in maltreatment cases is the absence of a witness to the actual incident of abuse or neglect that caused the child's life-threatening or fatal injuries. Unlike other homicides, in which a person may be killed in a public place, maltreatment murders almost always occur in a private location, such as the family's home.

Accomplices are also rare in maltreatment cases. It is unusual for two or more people to participate in the child's fatal maltreatment. Far more common is the situation in which one person is aware that another (e.g., a spouse, girlfriend, or boyfriend) is abusing or neglecting a child but fails to report the maltreatment or take steps to protect the child. (The person who is aware of the abuse may actually interfere with the investigation by lying to investigators or tampering with physical evidence. If you suspect this is happening, consult your local prosecutor about any possible criminal charges.)

Although an investigation may not present an opportunity to turn two accomplices against each other, it may be possible to convince the person not actually involved in the abuse or neglect to testify about how the suspect treated the child. (More and more states are limiting spousal immunity in child abuse cases and other circumstances. Consult your local prosecutor for advice in these situations.) To obtain cooperation, it is often possible to charge a reluctant witness with failure to report suspected child abuse or failure to protect a child. In some cases, these individuals may actually have been involved in the fatal maltreatment and can be charged as accomplices in the child's death.

Weapons

Maltreatment murders of children rarely involve traditional weapons (i.e., firearms, knives, blunt objects). Typical weapons include hands, feet, household items, and scalding water. Often, death results from injuries caused by shaking, slamming, blunt force trauma, scalding, starvation, neglectful supervision, and various other forms of physical abuse and neglect. The investigation is unlikely to turn up a weapon that will directly link the offender to the crime in the way that ballistic evidence links a suspect's gun to a victim's death. The exception may be a human bite mark or an instrument such as an electrical extension cord that leaves a distinctive pattern injury.

Trace Evidence

In most cases of fatal child maltreatment, trace evidence such as fingerprints and DNA will be of far less value than it might be in other crimes. For example, if a child who lives with both parents is beaten to death at home, the mere presence of the parents' fingerprints at the scene links neither of them to the crime. Exceptions are cases in which the offender sexually assaulted or bit the child and DNA evidence is involved.

Circumstantial Evidence

Because most fatal child maltreatment cases lack witnesses or any direct evidence tying a specific individual to the crime, these cases may often depend on circumstantial evidence. Your investigation must prove that only the suspect could have committed the crime. Two critically important steps are (1) to establish that the suspect was the *only* person with the child at the time of the fatal injury and (2) to prove that the injury was *not* accidental.

Internal Injuries

In many child fatalities, the victim's injuries may not be visible at first. The symptoms or signs of some injuries may begin to appear hours or days after the child sustained the injuries. Most fatal injuries of children involve trauma to the brain and the internal organs of the abdomen and chest. These injuries can only be detected with medical procedures such as x rays, CT and MRI scans, and the forensic autopsy. Unless the child's injuries are visible externally, the death may appear natural at first. During the investigation, you must not jump to conclusions based solely on an external examination of the child's body. This is especially true for an infant whose death may appear to be from natural causes such as SIDS.

Motives

Child maltreatment murders are, by definition, committed by persons responsible for the care and supervision of the victim. In 2001, an estimated 83 percent of these fatalities involved a parent, and 17 percent involved a nonparent caretaker. The motives in these cases differ from those typically found in homicide cases. Caretakers generally do not kill their children for revenge or greed or during the commission of a violent crime such as a robbery or sexual assault. (This is not to say that on occasion, children cannot be murdered by sadistic, violent, or mentally disturbed caretakers.) In many child fatalities, the victim is subjected to violent assault because of crying, bedwetting, or feeding problems or because the caretaker has feelings of resentment, frustration, or hatred for the child.

Legal Responsibility in Accidental Deaths

The fact that a child's death is classified as accidental does not necessarily mean that an investigation is not required. In cases involving a child's accidental death that may have resulted from a caretaker's neglect, the investigation must prove two things: (1) that the caretaker failed to act reasonably in providing care or supervision and (2) that this failure resulted in the child's death. The accidental death of a child involves issues not present in the accidental death of an adult. When an adult's death is accidental, usually no other person is criminally responsible (except in cases involving driving while intoxicated and in certain other situations provided for by statute). When, for example, an unsupervised child drowns in a backyard swimming pool, the child's parent or caretaker could face criminal charges, depending on the circumstances surrounding the event. State laws define the legal responsibility for parents or for other caretakers who act *in loco parentis* (in place of parents) to properly supervise children under their care.

Other Considerations

Suspected maltreatment in deaths not attributed to abuse or neglect. Occasionally, an autopsy finds evidence of prior abuse or neglect when a child has died from natural, accidental, or undetermined causes. In such cases, it is important to report suspected maltreatment as you would report it were the child still living. Not only is it possible that a crime was committed and can be proven, reporting suspected maltreatment is necessary to protect any surviving children from being harmed by the caretaker or caretakers involved.

Daycare centers and babysitters. When a child dies from abuse while in the custody of a licensed (or unlicensed) daycare center or babysitter, the investigator's challenge is to determine whether the acting caretaker committed fatal abuse or the child's parents committed abuse that resulted in delayed death. Law enforcement has sole responsibility for investigating the criminal aspects of such deaths but should also involve the appropriate licensing agency to address licensure issues and protect other children.

Undetermined cause and manner of death. When the cause and manner of a child's death are classified as undetermined, an investigation may still be in order. However, you should realize that the physical findings from deaths due to suffocation and SIDS may appear the same at autopsy and may be hard to differentiate. Occasionally, you may not know for certain whether you are dealing with a caretaker who has lost a child to SIDS or one who actually murdered the child. In some cases, you will never know (or be able to prove conclusively) what happened to a child.

Children as suspects. A child's fatal injuries may have been caused by another child in the home. The investigation should take this possibility into account.

The Roles of Child Protective Services and Law Enforcement

Another unusual aspect of child fatality cases is the involvement of an agency other than law enforcement—CPS—in the investigation. CPS has legal authority to be involved in the investigation of a child's death when a parent or other member of the household is suspected. However, the CPS role is very different from the law enforcement role.

The role of CPS is to determine whether maltreatment was involved in the child's death, identify the responsible party, and then take appropriate action to protect any surviving siblings. CPS does not determine whether anyone committed a crime. CPS personnel are not trained as criminal investigators nor are they trained to collect evidence or interrogate suspected offenders. Therefore, it is important that law enforcement and CPS communicate and coordinate their efforts during the investigation. One coordinated investigation is always preferable to two separate investigations. In fact, at least 30 states have either mandated or authorized implementation of multidisciplinary teams to investigate child maltreatment.

Your role as the law enforcement investigator is to determine (1) whether a crime has been committed and (2) who is responsible. Accomplishing this involves analyzing old and new injuries revealed by an autopsy and by a review of the child's medical history, thoroughly investigating the death scene, collecting and examining evidence, interviewing witnesses, and interrogating suspects.

Although it is important that law enforcement and CPS coordinate their efforts, *it is imperative that law enforcement assume the leadership role in the investigation.* This is necessary because of the legal and practical issues involved in obtaining evidence and confessions. Only a law enforcement investigator has the training, expertise, and legal mandate to execute search warrants, collect and evaluate evidence, interrogate suspects, and file criminal charges. If a CPS investigator prematurely confronts a parent suspected of fatally abusing a child, the law enforcement investigator will find it more difficult, if not impossible, to successfully interrogate that same individual at a later date.

Remember that law enforcement and CPS investigators are both acting under statutory requirements. Only if law enforcement and CPS coordinate their efforts and use their respective resources and skills collaboratively will the investigation succeed.

Conducting the Child Fatality Investigation

Although most sudden and unexpected deaths of children are not caused by abuse and neglect, you should approach every investigation with the hypothesis that the child may have been a victim of maltreatment. Maintain this position until the investigation is completed and the evidence conclusively proves otherwise. With this open approach, you guard against jumping to unsubstantiated conclusions or focusing the investigation too narrowly on what first appears to be the cause of death. Although this approach may appear biased toward suspecting the worst of parents and caretakers, it will ensure that you preserve evidence and witness statements early in the investigation. Documenting the events in question will prove very important if the investigation finds that the case does involve maltreatment.

To understand the importance of this open approach, consider the example of one element of the investigation: handling witnesses. With the open approach, you will interview parents, caretakers, and other witnesses—even if the child's death appears to be of natural causes—*before* the autopsy is conducted and a final ruling is issued. If you wait until after the autopsy, and the autopsy finds evidence of maltreatment, you will have lost valuable investigative time (and possibly evidence), and the offender will have had the opportunity to rehearse or coordinate statements and destroy or tamper with evidence.

Only by initially entertaining *every possible explanation* for the child's death can you be sure to ultimately identify the correct one. However, you should never in any way communicate suspicion of maltreatment to the victim's parents, witnesses, or anyone under investigation until the medical examiner's ruling on cause and manner of death supports this position. More often than not, the investigation will reveal that the child died of causes other than maltreatment.

A professionally conducted child fatality investigation consists of several important elements, discussed in the next sections. Each element is an integral part of the investigation. None is independent of the others; in fact, some elements often build on others as the investigation proceeds. For example, information learned in processing the crime scene influences how you interview witnesses and interrogate the suspect. Properly implemented, each element contributes to a successful investigation.

Coordinating the Response

The investigation usually begins when a law enforcement or CPS agency receives notification of a child's death or life-threatening injury. At that point, it is very important that investigators from both agencies coordinate their efforts. Coordination ensures that each agency's investigators make informed decisions from the outset about the probability of maltreatment and the implications for the required response. For example, if maltreatment is suspected, you may have to secure a search warrant to look for evidence at the child's residence, and the CPS investigator may have to pursue the emergency removal of surviving siblings.

To facilitate a coordinated response, government agencies and hospitals must notify the appropriate law enforcement and CPS agencies immediately whenever there is a sudden and unexplained child death or life-threatening injury. They should have policies that specifically outline when and to whom notification should be made. This notification may come from the first patrol officers or paramedics who arrive at the scene or from medical staff at the hospital where the child is transported.

Law enforcement and CPS agencies conducting joint investigations must follow any state law regarding cross-reporting (the exchange of initial reports of suspected abuse and neglect that each agency receives). They must also observe any investigative protocol—specific procedures for investigating abuse and neglect—in effect. For example, the protocol may provide that CPS interviews all child witnesses and law enforcement interviews all adult witnesses.

Arriving on the Scene: The Responsibilities of First Responders

Law enforcement officers dispatched to the location of a seriously injured or deceased child—the "first responders" on the scene—have several important responsibilities to carry out before the investigators arrive. (This assumes that paramedics have already reached the scene and are attending to the child.)

* The officers' first priority is to identify and secure the potential crime scene or location where the child was injured or discovered. It is important to remember that the scene may involve more than one room in a house and may also involve the outdoors.

* Officers then should assess the situation and request additional support as necessary, including more officers to help secure the scene, crisis counselors, paramedics, personnel from the coroner's or medical examiner's office, and the detectives or investigators who will conduct the investigation.

* First responders should clear all individuals from the scene and make sure that nobody enters the area where they could tamper with or remove evidence. This can be difficult because family members may be very emotional and may not want to leave the deceased child. Patience and diplomacy will encourage cooperation from family members.

* While securing the scene, first responders should be observant. They should look at what is happening and listen to what people are saying. Until the officers have time to write down their observations, they should make mental notes of anything that may be relevant.

* Without attempting to conduct thorough interviews of the parents or other caretakers, the first responders should identify who discovered the child and then find out whether anyone attempted first aid or moved, dressed, or bathed the child. The officers should give this information to the investigators as soon as they arrive.

* Once the scene is secure, one officer should be charged with maintaining a log of all personnel who enter the scene. The first

responders should also ensure that nobody opens or closes windows, uses the commode, or disposes of anything (trash, the child's clothing, medicine, or anything else) until the scene has been processed and photographed.

* Until the investigator or detective arrives, the first responders should obtain the names of those present and their relationship to the child. The officers should allow no one to leave the location until this information is obtained.

Collecting Evidence

If you suspect that a child's life-threatening injuries or death may be the result of maltreatment, you must act immediately to preserve the crime scene and then collect any evidence. Evidence collection includes photographing the victim and searching the location where you believe the injuries occurred. *Before searching any possible crime scene, be sure to determine whether a search warrant or consent to search is necessary.* If you have any doubts, consult your legal advisor. In most child death cases, there is no exception to the fourth amendment requirement for a search warrant or a valid consent to search.

Include the following in the search of the scene:

* Ensure that scale diagrams are made of the layout and that photographs and/or a video are taken. Photographs should show the general location and progress to specific items of interest.

* Consider as evidence prescription or over-the-counter medicine the child was taking and other medicine or substances the child may have ingested. If it is not practical to remove such medicine from the scene (e.g., because someone else in the household needs it), document the information on the label.

* If it appears that the child may have died of malnourishment, you may want to make an inventory of the amount of baby food or formula that is present. Document and photograph what you find.

* If you find evidence of the caretaker's alcohol and/or substance abuse, carefully document and photograph your findings. Take appropriate legal action if you find illegal drugs or drug paraphernalia.

* Search trash cans inside and outside the residence for possible evidence, such as bloodstained clothing; items used to clean up blood, vomit, urine, or feces; and implements used to injure the child, such as wooden spoons, belts, and electrical extension cords.

Gathering Information

Prosecution of fatal maltreatment cases often depends heavily on medical evidence, which can involve confusing, technical material that may be difficult for a jury to understand. This may include testimony and opinions of several medical specialists, such as emergency room doctors, pediatricians, surgeons, radiologists, and forensic pathologists. Sometimes, a "battle of the medical experts" will largely determine a defendant's fate in criminal proceedings. The question of innocence or guilt may be reduced to which medical expert the jury believes.

It is your responsibility to gather additional information and evidence that reduces the jury's reliance on medical testimony and the opinions of medical experts. This information can be anything that either supports or refutes a caretaker's explanation for the child's injuries. During this phase of the investigation, you interview witnesses, collect background information, and review 911 records and autopsy results.

Interviewing Witnesses

Conducting timely, thorough interviews of witnesses contributes greatly to the success of a child fatality investigation. The list of potential witnesses varies from case to case but usually includes the deceased child's siblings and parents, the child's caretakers immediately prior to the death or during the time the child appeared to be in medical distress, neighbors, law enforcement first responders, paramedics, medical providers, and anyone else who may have relevant information about the child or the events leading to the injury or death.

An interview is not the same as an interrogation, and it is important to understand the difference. An interview is a nonconfrontational conversation between two people in which information is exchanged. By contrast, an interrogation is an attempt to obtain a confession from a suspect who is believed to have committed a crime (as discussed later in this guide). In an interview, the person being questioned may have knowledge the investigator needs. Because the person is not under arrest and formal charges have not been filed, it usually is not necessary to give Miranda warnings at this point. (Some jurisdictions may require investigators to give Miranda warnings to anyone who has become the focus of an investigation. Ask your district attorney or department legal advisor about the policy you should follow.)

Keep in mind the following considerations as you interview witnesses in child fatality investigations:

* **Conduct interviews as early in the investigation as practical.** Even though interviewing parents and caretakers in these situations can be difficult, it is preferable to interview them sooner rather than later.

* Whenever possible, **interview witnesses separately.**

* Be careful to **distinguish between what a witness actually observed and knows firsthand and what someone else may have told the witness.** For example, if a witness states that a child fell from the couch, it is important to determine whether

---

Checklist of Potential Witnesses

❑ Parents (including current and former stepparents and parent's boyfriend or girlfriend).

❑ Siblings and other children.

❑ Family members.

❑ Caretakers (babysitters, childcare employees).

❑ Teachers (daycare, preschool, school, church).

❑ Neighbors (current and previous).

❑ First responders (police and emergency medical technicians).

❑ Emergency room personnel (physicians and nurses).

❑ Medical providers (providers who have seen the child previously, including school nurses).

❑ Agency personnel (CPS, daycare licensing, or law enforcement personnel who had previous contact with the family, the child, or any witnesses or possible suspects).

---

the witness actually saw the child fall or is just repeating some-one else's version of what happened. If the investigation later reveals that the child did not fall from the couch, the person who told the witness that this happened may actually have caused the child's injury—as demonstrated by giving false information to conceal his or her actions.

* After a witness gives a verbal account, **get a formal statement.** This applies to caretakers, neighbors, first responders, para-medics, medical professionals, and anyone else who has infor-mation about the event. Record the statement electronically (audio or videotape), or ask the witness to write or type it in affidavit format and then have the witness sign it. The value of the formal statement is that it documents the witness's version of events and locks the witness into that story. You can then verify or disprove that account in the investigation. A person originally viewed as a witness may later be identified as a sus-pect. Having the documentation of the formal statement pre-vents that person from changing his or her story as additional facts emerge.

* **Other children in the home of the deceased child—siblings, cousins, friends—often are important witnesses.** They may have observed or heard something directly related to the death, may have knowledge of the child's prior maltreatment, and may even know who is responsible. Because defense attorneys later may attack the credibility of witnesses, someone who has spe-cific training in how to interview children should conduct all interviews of child witnesses. If you do not have this training, find someone who does to interview the children for you. (Staff of children's advocacy centers, child death review teams, CPS, or victim witness programs may be able to suggest qualified interview specialists.) Even if children are too young to testify in court, they may provide information that can give investiga-tors a possible lead or direction for the investigation. Everyone involved in the investigation of a child's death must remember that the death of a loved one deeply affects surviving siblings and other children. These children should receive therapy and support from the appropriate agencies and professionals.

* **Refrain from making assumptions or drawing conclusions based on a witness's attitude, behavior, or emotional state during the interview.** Realize that people are going to act dif-ferently in a situation as emotionally charged as the death of a

child. The fact that a witness does or does not appear upset is not necessarily a true indication of whether that person was responsible for the child's death. Sometimes people who "appear" guilty are innocent, and vice versa.

* In the early stages of the investigation, **remember that your role is to *get information, not give it.*** Don't share what you have learned with the witnesses because that can influence their statements and willingness to cooperate. They could also share any information you give them with someone who is later identified as the suspect.

* In conducting an interview, **allow the witness to provide a narrative account** of what he or she actually knows about the event under investigation. For example, in a case where a child was brought to the hospital after suffering a seizure, consider asking the parent to tell everything that happened to the child in the previous 72 hours. Do not interrupt with questions or requests to repeat part of the account. This may be difficult, but it is better to hear the entire story and then ask about things that were not mentioned or need clarification. Conclude by asking if there is anything the witness forgot to mention or thinks you should know. Keep in mind that witnesses often do not volunteer information; if you want specific information, you must ask for it. Be careful about leading and suggestive questioning that implies your theory of the case.

* In some situations, it may be appropriate to request that a witness or a possible suspect take a **polygraph test.** Although the results are not admissible in court, they can be useful in subsequent interviews and interrogations. Be aware that most polygraph examiners will not conduct a test on the same day that an individual has already been interviewed or interrogated.

Collecting Background Information

Every child fatality investigation benefits from having as much background information as possible on the deceased child, the child's siblings and parents, and any caretakers or witnesses who were present at the time of death or during the 72 hours before the child was injured or found to be in need of medical attention. Sources of potentially important background information include the following:

* **Prior CPS reports or investigations involving the child, siblings, parents, and caretakers.** Remember that CPS records for a child are often filed under the mother's name. Check

records in all states where the involved parties have previously lived. (While interviewing witnesses, ask them where else they have lived and when.) A witness's involvement in an abuse case in another state could be very important information for your current case.

* **Law enforcement records on all witnesses and potential suspects.** In addition to conducting criminal history and wanted-person checks, determine whether individuals are or ever have been the subject of a protective order for spousal abuse. Keep in mind that some states do not submit protective orders to the National Crime Information Center (NCIC) system. (For additional information, contact NCIC at 304–625–2000.) Again, remember to check in all states where individuals have previously lived. In addition, check for police service calls to suspects' current and previous addresses regarding disturbances, domestic violence, or the welfare of children.

* **Medical records for the deceased child's entire life.** Secure the records and have a medical professional review them for any signs of prior abuse or neglect and any preexisting medical problems. Members of child death review teams (medical examiners, coroners, doctors, and prosecutors) may be of assistance in reviewing medical records. Look at birth records, growth charts, x rays, regular pediatrician checkups, and any records of emergency room treatment. Remember that access to medical records is governed by both state law and federal law (the Health Insurance Portability and Accountability Act, known as HIPAA). Consult with your legal advisor or prosecutor regarding court orders, subpoenas, or search warrants required to obtain medical records.

* **Insurance policies.** Determine whether a life insurance policy has been taken out on the deceased child and, if so, how much the policy is worth. Collecting on an insurance policy can be a motive in the murder of a child, although it is not a very common one.

Reviewing 911 Emergency Calls

A 911 call for assistance in the child fatality case under investigation may provide important information about the event. Keep in mind that more than one call may have come in about the same incident. The 911 computer records indicate the exact time and location of the call. Most 911 systems electronically record the conversations. You can listen to an audio copy of the call and hear exactly what the caller said. Often in maltreatment deaths, the caller actually caused the child's injuries, and there will be significant discrepancies between what that person said in the 911 call and what he or she says later in an interview. The 911 call will also help to determine the following:

* **Identity.** Even if the caller does not give a name, you may recognize the voice during a subsequent interview. In some cases, in which callers left the scene before first responders arrived, the recorded calls were the only proof they were at the location and somehow involved.

* **Reason for calling.** The caller may have said whether the child was sick, injured, unconscious, or deceased. Callers may contradict themselves in a subsequent interview.

* **Exact words.** Listen to how the caller describes the child's condition and the events and circumstances leading up to the phone call (e.g., the child fell down a flight of stairs and is now unconscious, or the caller found the child unconscious and knows nothing about the cause).

Checklist of Potential Information Sources

❏ CPS records (for the deceased child, siblings, or other children that the child's caretakers have been involved with).

❏ Law enforcement records (criminal history, victim or suspect history, calls for service).

❏ Medical records for the deceased child and siblings (birth, prenatal care, pediatrician, medical, emergency room).

❏ 911 calls.

❏ Emergency medical services (EMS) reports.

❏ Telephone calls that the suspect made or received around the time of the child's death (including cell phones, pagers, or messages on answering machines).

❏ Autopsy results.

Remember: Important records documenting a history of abuse or neglect may exist in cities, towns, or states where the child's family or the suspect previously lived.

---

* **Emotional state.** Tone of voice and choice of words may reveal the caller's emotional state. The caller may express remorse for his or her actions.

* **Other people at the location.** It may be possible to determine whether other people were present when the call was made. Even if they do not talk on the phone, the caller may talk to them or mention their names or their voices may be audible in the background.

Know the procedures of your 911 emergency call center or agency dispatcher. Almost all agencies erase tapes or digital recordings of emergency calls after a certain period of time, so be sure to obtain copies before the recordings you need are destroyed. (Again, keep in mind that more than one person may have called 911 about the incident in question, or the same person may have called more than once.) After obtaining a copy from the call center, make a backup copy for work purposes and keep the original copy in the file. If you are using a cassette tape, remove the tabs that allow a tape to be recorded to prevent accidentally taping over the conversation you need. You may also consider having a written transcript made of the 911 call, which will make it easier to locate specific statements during subsequent interviews and interrogations.

Learning From the Autopsy

The autopsy will determine the official cause of death (blunt force trauma, drowning, etc.) and manner of death (natural, accidental, homicide, suicide, undetermined). You should observe the autopsy if at all possible. The information learned from the autopsy will better prepare you for subsequent interviews and interrogations.

The pathologist can provide information about the child's injuries, including those related to the death and those previously inflicted, and about the child's general state of health prior to death. It is important to ask the pathologist to explain whether a single event or multiple factors caused or contributed to the death. Additionally, based on the injuries, the pathologist or a pediatrician may be able to say how the child would have reacted after being injured—e.g., whether the child would have been able to walk or talk, been in obvious pain, or lost consciousness. Another important question to ask is when the child's symptoms would have first appeared. The answers to these questions may help you determine whether witness accounts are truthful.

In turn, you can tell the pathologist what you have learned from your interviews and record checks. In many cases, the pathologist can offer an opinion regarding the possibility that the child's injuries occurred in the manner described by witnesses. The pathologist may also be able to estimate the time of death, based on stomach contents and your notes about the child's last meal.

Documenting the Case

The official case file must document the entire investigation—from the time law enforcement received the initial call to the time criminal charges are filed. It must include copies of all official police reports, investigators' notes, medical records, the autopsy report and pictures, crime scene pictures, the 911 recordings, witness statements, search warrants, newspaper articles, background information on the suspect, and any other relevant information or records obtained during the investigation.

Because most of the information in the official file will be subject to the defense attorney's discovery, you need to be thoroughly familiar with the file's contents. A defense attorney may attempt to impeach your testimony on the witness stand by obtaining statements from you that contradict the evidence in the case file.

In entering notes in the case file, refrain from including your lay opinions (i.e., ideas outside the scope of your professional knowledge) about things like time of death, body temperature, cause of death, etc., if these opinions contradict or are not supported by evidence in the case. Finally, check the CPS investigator's case file for items that should be in the law enforcement case file but are not. (As you review the CPS file, keep in mind that you may be questioned about real or imagined discrepancies between the CPS and law enforcement files. Also remember that any documents you release to CPS—witness statements, police reports, etc.—may be subject to discovery in civil legal proceedings.)

Interrogating Suspects

In a child fatality case, proper interrogation of a suspect may be instrumental in identifying the person responsible for the child's injuries. Unless there is a videotape of the fatal maltreatment (which is almost never the case), a suspect's voluntary confession of guilt is probably the most powerful evidence that can be presented at trial. However, a suspect's written or electronically recorded voluntary statement is of little value unless it is admitted into evidence. The defense attorney will almost always challenge a suspect's confession by claiming coercion or some other violation of the client's rights under the 4th, 5th, 6th, or 14th constitutional amendment. Therefore, you must be thoroughly familiar with the case law in your state as it relates to obtaining confessions and the admissibility of confessions as evidence.

Ensure and *carefully document* that the suspect's constitutional rights are protected and that all applicable departmental procedures and state laws are followed. At a minimum, the case file should contain the following documentation:

* Whether the suspect was under arrest at the time of the interrogation or was just brought in for questioning.

* When the interrogation started and how long it lasted.

* How often and at what time the suspect was allowed to use the restroom or to have something to eat or drink.

* The names of any individuals who participated in the interrogation or observed it.

* Whether the suspect had any physical impairments or medical problems that could interfere with the ability to speak, hear, or understand what was being said. (If a person is legally deaf, state law may require the presence of a certified sign language interpreter.)

* The suspect's level of formal education and whether the suspect can read and write.

When dealing with juvenile suspects, be certain that you know and follow every applicable departmental policy and state law, and be sure to document your actions. Some states require additional legal safeguards for juvenile suspects, such as the presence of an attorney or parents during interrogation.

Interrogate the suspect as early in the investigation as possible. You can usually begin as soon as the cause and manner of death are known (even if the official autopsy report has not been written) and the evidence indicates who the suspect is. In some situations, it may be best to interrogate the suspect before the autopsy is conducted (see "Learning From the Autopsy," above). The following guidelines will assist in conducting a proper interrogation.

* Dress in business or casual clothes, not in a uniform. Do not wear a badge or carry a gun or handcuffs.

* If the suspect does not speak English and an interpreter is needed, make sure the interpreter is an expert in the suspect's language. This applies even when a law enforcement officer is used as an interpreter. Some states require that an individual pass a qualification test to be certified as an interpreter for legal proceedings. The defense attorney may challenge the proficiency of any person used as an interpreter during an interrogation. An interpreter's incorrect use of one word can change the entire meaning of a sentence.

* Have another investigator observe the interrogation.

  ● If your agency does not videotape interrogations, the observer can rebut any allegations that you mistreated the suspect or coerced a confession.

  ● If you cannot obtain a confession, the other investigator will be prepared to speak to the suspect. Observation allows the other investigator to know what the suspect has said and to reinforce, not contradict, what you have said. This "second bite at the apple" often results in a confession.

* Even if you cannot obtain a confession, document everything the suspect says. A suspect who does not confess to causing the child's fatal injuries may offer an explanation of the injuries and surrounding events that is implausible or can be refuted by evidence. By documenting this unlikely account during the interrogation, you in effect lock the suspect into a story that can later be disproved or that will make the individual appear deceptive if he or she testifies in court.

Always keep in mind that even if a suspect confesses, the confession may be suppressed at trial for a variety of procedural and legal reasons. That is one reason **you must not stop working on the case even if you obtain a confession.** Continue to investigate any new leads and interview anyone you think may have relevant information.

Testifying in Court

If the investigation of a child fatality case leads to legal proceedings (grand jury, preliminary hearing, or criminal trial), you will be responsible for testifying about how the investigation was conducted. Because your testimony will be essential in convincing a judge or jury that the investigation was thorough and reliable, you must present yourself as an experienced, competent professional. The following advice can help you accomplish that.

* **Be prepared.** Before being called to testify in any proceeding, make sure you know the facts of the case and what you will be expected to testify about. The prosecutor will usually meet with you before a trial to review your testimony and the facts of the case. If the prosecutor does not schedule such a pretrial meeting, you should request one.

* **Be truthful.** It may seem obvious that you should testify truthfully. However, defense attorneys will ask certain questions that can cause an investigator to become confused and hesitant to answer:

  * "Have you discussed your testimony with anyone before testifying today?" If you have discussed your testimony with the prosecutor, just say so. Most people in a courtroom know that good prosecutors spend time with their witnesses before trial. If the defense attorney implies that the prosecutor told you what to say, your answer should convey to the jury that the prosecutor's only instructions were for you to be truthful and accurate in your testimony.

  * "Isn't it true, detective, that you lied to my client during the interrogation?" If the defendant confessed during your interrogation, you can count on the defense attorney asking a question like this. Again, if you lied to the suspect, just say so. Lying to a suspect in the interrogation room is a common law enforcement technique and many legal precedents support the concept that deception is often necessary for effective law enforcement. Ideally, the prosecutor's followup questions will allow you to make it clear to the jury that you understand the difference between the need to deceive suspects in the interrogation room and the need to testify truthfully in the courtroom.

* **Review the case file.** Be thorough. Know exactly what the file does and does not contain. If necessary, ask the judge if you may refer to your notes before answering a question. Pay special attention to the chronology of events. Prepare a timeline of important events. You will be asked what you did, when, and why. When you look at the crime scene photographs, try to picture yourself at the scene. You may be asked where various items were located in respect to others. Be sure to review all statements provided by witnesses and the defendant.

* **Appearance.** Dress in appropriate business attire or in uniform. Turn off your cell phone or pager. Your duty weapon should not be visible (unless you are in uniform).

* **Never argue with the defense attorney.** The defense attorney will try to show that you did not conduct a professional investigation (which would mean that the defendant must be innocent). The attorney may use facial expressions, body language, and tough questions to accomplish this. Although your professionalism and integrity may be challenged, do not lose your composure. If you are disrespectful, unresponsive, or sarcastic, you will get in trouble with the judge and diminish the value of your testimony.

* **Be confident.** When appropriate, use positive terms that convey the conviction of your answer. Avoid using qualifying statements, such as "I think" or "I believe." If you know the answer, just give it. If you don't know the answer, say so. A common tactic for defense attorneys is to ask "If you had it to do over, could you have done a more thorough investigation?" If that is not true, say that you conducted a thorough investigation. Convey your confidence in the investigation and your professionalism to the jury.

* **Attend the final arguments.** During the trial, you probably will be allowed in the courtroom only when you testify. However, once the prosecutor and the defense rest their cases, you will probably be allowed to be present for the final arguments. Your presence tells the jury that you are interested in the outcome of the case. In addition, you can hear what both sides believe to be the strongest and weakest evidence in the case. This is an opportunity for you to learn what you did well and what you can improve in your next investigation.

* **Talk to the prosecutor.** An excellent way to improve your courtroom testimony is to ask the prosecutor for feedback. In addition to providing personal observations about your testimony, the prosecutor may be able to offer you suggestions for improvement.

Conclusion

As a law enforcement officer responsible for investigating the death of a child, you have an important responsibility. You must speak for the child. If the death was attributable to abuse or neglect, you must help society identify those responsible and hold

Tips and Reminders for
Law Enforcement Investigators

1. Many child fatalities are initially reported as accidents or natural deaths.

2. An unreasonable delay in seeking medical attention is often a "red flag" that the child's injuries may have been caused by abuse.

3. Records of 911 calls often contain important information about what people originally reported regarding the child's injuries.

4. It is not uncommon for severely injured children to die days or weeks after the original injury. Treat cases involving severe injury as potential child fatalities.

5. Delayed deaths often involve more than one crime scene. Examine the place where the injury occurred, the hospital where the child died, and any private vehicle used to transport the child to the hospital.

6. Coordinate and communicate with CPS investigators in child fatality cases. They have a legitimate role in the investigation, and they often have important information on the child and the family involved.

7. Do not automatically exclude children as potential suspects. Children have been known to inflict severe injuries on other children.

8. The three keys to a successful child fatality investigation are effectively conducted, well documented interviews of witnesses; careful background checks of everyone involved; and competent interrogation of the suspect(s).

9. There is no substitute for a timely, professional crime scene search, including evidence collection, documentation, and photodocumentation.

10. If criminal charges are filed, properly prepare for your courtroom testimony and deliver it competently.

them accountable for their actions. Your efforts serve not only to ensure that justice is done in this case, but also to protect other children from future victimization at the hands of the abuser. If the death was not attributable to maltreatment, you must see that innocent people are not improperly suspected, arrested, charged, or convicted. It is the goal of this guide to assist you in this most important work.

Author

Lieutenant Bill Walsh (Retired)
Crimes Against Children Unit
Special Investigations Division
Reserve Battalion
Dallas Police Department
1400 South Lamar Street
Dallas TX 75215
214–671–4214
waldo4122@grandecom.net

Supplemental Reading

Many of the other publications in OJJDP's Portable Guides to Investigating Child Abuse Series contain information relevant to investigating child fatality cases. (See "Other Titles in This Series," page 30.) The following publications also offer useful information:

American Prosecutors Research Institute (APRI), National Center for Prosecution of Child Abuse. *Investigation and Prosecution of Child Abuse.* 3d ed. Thousand Oaks, CA: Sage Publications, Inc., 2004.

Bonner BL, Crow SM, Louge MB. Fatal child neglect. In Dubowitz H (ed): *Neglected Children.* Thousand Oaks, CA: Sage Publications, Inc., 2002, pp. 156–173.

Briere J, Berliner L, Bulkley JA, Jenny C, Reid T (eds). *The APSAC Handbook on Child Maltreatment.* 2d ed. Thousand Oaks, CA: Sage Publications, Inc., 1998.

Cook N, Hermann M. *Criminal Defense Checklists.* Deerfield, IL: CBC, 1996.

Kochanek KD, Smith BL. Deaths: Preliminary data for 2002. *National Vital Statistics Reports* 52(13):27, 2002.

Myers JEB. *Legal Issues in Child Abuse and Neglect.* Newbury Park, CA: Sage Publications, Inc., 1992.

National Clearinghouse on Child Abuse and Neglect Information (NCCANI). *Child Abuse and Neglect Fatalities: Statistics and Interventions.* Fact Sheet. Washington, DC: U.S. Department of Health and Human Services, Administration for Children and Families, NCCANI, August 2003.

Peddle N, Wang CT, Diaz J, Reid R. *Current Trends in Child Abuse Prevention and Fatalities: The 2000 Fifty State Survey.* Working Paper 808. Chicago, IL: Prevent Child Abuse America, National Center on Child Abuse Prevention Research, September 2002.

Pence D, Wilson C. *Team Investigation of Child Sexual Abuse.* Thousand Oaks, CA: Sage Publications, Inc., 1994.

Pomponio AT (ed). *Investigation and Prosecution of Child Abuse.* 3d ed. Thousand Oaks, CA: Sage Publications, Inc., 2004.

Reece RM (ed). *Child Abuse: Medical Diagnosis and Management.* Malvern, PA: Lea and Febiger, 1994.

Whitcomb D. *When the Victim Is a Child.* 2d ed. Washington, DC: U.S. Department of Justice, Office of Justice Programs, National Institute of Justice, 1992.

Zulawski DE, Wicklander DE. *Practical Aspects of Interview and Interrogation.* Boca Raton, Fl: CRC Press, 1993.

Organizations

Missing and Exploited Children's Training Programs
Fox Valley Technical College
Criminal Justice Division
Child Protection Training Center
1825 North Bluemound Drive
P.O. Box 2277
Appleton, WI 54913–2277
800–648–4966
920–735–4757 (fax)
dept.fvtc.edu/ojjdp

Participants are trained in child abuse and exploitation investigative techniques, covering the following areas:

* Recognition of signs of abuse.

* Collection and preservation of evidence.

* Preparation of cases for prosecution.

* Techniques for interviewing victims and offenders.

* Liability issues.

Fox Valley also offers intensive special training for local child investigative teams. Teams must include representatives from law enforcement, prosecution, social services, and (optionally) the medical field. Participants take part in hands-on team activity involving:

* Development of interagency processes and protocols for enhanced enforcement, prevention, and intervention in child abuse cases.

* Case preparation and prosecution.

* Development of the team's own interagency implementation plan for improved investigation of child abuse.

National Center on Child Fatality Review
4024 North Durfee Avenue
El Monte, CA 91732
626–455–4585
626–444–4581 (fax)
www.ican-ncfr.org

The mission of NCFR is to develop and promote a nationwide system of child fatality review teams to improve the health, safety, and well-being of children and reduce preventable child fatalities. The NCFR Web site includes material on child deaths, contact information for child fatality review teams, current studies and articles, and links to other useful sites.

National Center for Prosecution of Child Abuse
American Prosecutors Research Institute (APRI)
99 Canal Center Plaza, Suite 510
Alexandria, VA 22314
703–549–9222
703–836–3195 (fax)
www.ndaa-apri.org/apri/programs/ncpca/ncpca_home.html

The National Center for Prosecution of Child Abuse is a nonprofit and technical assistance affiliate of APRI. In addition to research and technical assistance, the Center provides extensive training on the investigation and prosecution of child abuse and child deaths. The national trainings include timely information presented by a variety of professionals experienced in the medical, legal, and investigative aspects of child abuse.

National Center on Shaken Baby Syndrome
2955 Harrison Boulevard, #102
Ogden, UT 84403
801–627–3399
888–273–0071
801–627–3321 (fax)
www.dontshake.com

The National Center on Shaken Baby Syndrome is a private, non-profit corporation that gathers information through national research surveys and by working closely with recognized experts in the field. The Center also educates professionals and family members on the prevention, investigation, and prosecution of shaken baby syndrome.

Other Titles in This Series

Currently there are 13 other Portable Guides to Investigating Child Abuse. To obtain a copy of any of the guides listed below (in order of publication), contact the Office of Juvenile Justice and Delinquency Prevention's Juvenile Justice Clearing-house by e-mail at puborder@ncjrs.org or by telephone at 800–851–3420

Recognizing When a Child's Injury or Illness Is Caused by Abuse, NCJ 160938

Sexually Transmitted Diseases and Child Sexual Abuse, NCJ 160940

Photodocumentation in the Investigation of Child Abuse, NCJ 160939

Diagnostic Imaging of Child Abuse, NCJ 161235

Battered Child Syndrome: Investigating Physical Abuse and Homicide, NCJ 161406

Interviewing Child Witnesses and Victims of Sexual Abuse, NCJ 161623

Child Neglect and Munchausen Syndrome by Proxy, NCJ 161841

Criminal Investigation of Child Sexual Abuse, NCJ 162426

Burn Injuries in Child Abuse, NCJ 162424

Law Enforcement Response to Child Abuse, NCJ 162425

Understanding and Investigating Child Sexual Exploitation, NCJ 162427

Use of Computers in the Sexual Exploitation of Children, NCJ 170021

Forming a Multidisciplinary Team To Investigate Child Abuse, NCJ 170020

Additional Resources

American Bar Association
  (ABA) Center on Children
  and the Law
Washington, D.C.
202–662–1720
www.abanet.org/child/home.html

American Humane Association
Englewood, Colorado
303–792–9900
www.americanhumane.org

American Medical Association
  (AMA)
Chicago, Illinois
800–621–8335
www.ama-assn.org

American Professional Society
  on the Abuse of Children
  (APSAC)
Charleston, South Carolina
877–402–7722
www.apsac.org

Federal Bureau of Investigation
  (FBI)
202–324–3000
www.fbi.gov

  *National Center for the
  Analysis of Violent Crime*
  www.fbi.gov/hq/isd/cirg/
    ncavc.htm

  *Crimes Against Children
  Program*
  www.fbi.gov/hq/cid/cac/
    crimesmain.htm

Juvenile Justice Clearinghouse
  (JJC)
Rockville, Maryland
800–851–3420
www.ojjdp.ncjrs.org/programs/
  ProgSummary.asp?pi=2

Kempe Children's Center
Denver, Colorado
303–864–5252
www.kempecenter.org

Missing and Exploited
  Children's Training Program
Fox Valley Technical College
Appleton, Wisconsin
800–648–4966
dept.fvtc.edu/ojjdp

National Association of
  Medical Examiners
Atlanta, Georgia
404–730–4781
www.thename.org

National Center for Missing
  and Exploited Children
  (NCMEC)
Alexandria, Virginia
800–THE–LOST
703–274–3900
www.missingkids.com

National Center for Prosecution
  of Child Abuse
Alexandria, Virginia
703–549–9222
www.ndaa-apri.org/apri/programs/
  ncpca/ncpca_home.html

National Children's Alliance
Washington, D.C.
800–239–9950
202–452–6001
www.nca-online.org

National Clearinghouse
  on Child Abuse and
  Neglect Information
Washington, D.C.
800–394–3366
703–385–7565
nccanch.acf.hhs.gov

National SIDS Resource Center
McLean, Virginia
866–866–7437
www.sidscenter.org

Prevent Child Abuse America
Chicago, Illinois
312–663–3520
www.preventchildabuse.org

www.ingramcontent.com/pod-product-compliance
Lightning Source LLC
Chambersburg PA
CBHW081136280526
45787CB00007B/3104